What's in this book

This book belongs to

_____

生病了 I'm sick!

学习内容 Contents

沟通 Communication

说说身体健康情况
Talk about physical health

背景介绍：
下雪了，伊森和艾文在家门口的花园里堆雪人。
但是艾文穿得很少。

生词 New words

★	生病	to be sick
★	看病	to see a doctor
★	生气	angry
★	医生	doctor
★	护士	nurse
★	药	medicine
★	等	to wait
★	应该	should
	讨厌	to hate
	健康	healthy
	打针	to have an injection

句式 Sentence patterns

我应该去看病。
I should see a doctor.

我们不应该淘气。
We should not be so naughty.

跨学科学习 Project

认识健康生活方式
Learn about the healthy lifestyle

文化 Cultures

传统中医
Traditional Chinese medicine

参考答案：

1 Yes, I exercise every day./No, I get sick quite often.
2 No, because I hate injections and medicine./No, but we should see a doctor if we are sick.
3 No, he should wear a coat. He might catch a cold.

Get ready

1 Are you healthy?

2 Do you like going to the doctor's when you are sick?

3 Do you think Ivan is dressed warm enough? What might happen?

读一读 Read

01

故事大意：
艾文生病了，妈妈要带他去看病，但他讨厌打针和吃药，于是就让哥哥依森代替他去看医生。妈妈发现后很生气，两兄弟知错并承认了错误。

kàn bìng
看病

tǎo yàn
讨厌

yào
药

dǎ zhēn
打针

艾文感冒了，妈妈要带他去看病，
但是他讨厌打针和吃药。

参考问题和答案：
Ivan does not feel well. What is he thinking about? (He is thinking about how he hated seeing the doctor because he hates injections and medicine.)

参考问题和答案：
1. What are the boys doing? (They are exchanging clothes with each other.)
2. Why do you think they do this? (Because Ethan is pretending to be Ivan and going to see the doctor.)
3. What is Ethan doing? (Ethan is waiting for Mum to take him to see the doctor.)

艾文不想去看病。伊森假装生病了，穿着弟弟的衣服等妈妈。

hù shi
护士

参考问题和答案：

1 Where are Ethan and Mum? (They are at a clinic.)

2 Why does Ethan look so nervous? (Because he is scared that Mum and the nurse might find out that he is not Ivan.)

3 Have Mum and the nurse noticed that it is Ethan and not Ivan? (No, they have not.)

"你是下一个，艾文。"护士叫病人的名字。伊森很紧张。

参考问题和答案：

1 What is the doctor doing? (He is doing a check-up on Ethan.)

2 Why does the doctor look confused? (Because he thinks Ethan is healthy. He is not sick.)

3 How does Mum look? (She looks shocked. She did not notice that Ethan came instead of Ivan.)

"他很健康，没生病。"医生向妈妈说。伊森脸红了，低下头。

shēng qì
生气

参考问题和答案：

1　How does Mum look? Why? (She looks angry because Ethan came to see the doctor instead of Ivan.)

2　How does Ethan look? Why? (He looks embarrassed because he helped Ivan in the wrong way.)

"对不起，医生，我弟弟讨厌看病，我代替他来。"伊森说。妈妈很生气。

"应该"表示在事实上、感情上或者道理上的需要。一般结构为"应该＋动作或行为"。如"我应该好好休息。"

yīng gāi
应该

参考问题和答案：

1 How does Ivan feel? (Ivan still feels sick.)
2 Do you think Ivan should go and see the doctor? (Yes, he should.)
3 Is Mum still angry with the boys? (No, because Ethan said that they should not be so naughty.)

"我应该去看病的。"艾文说。"对不起，妈妈，我们不应该淘气。"伊森说。

Let's think

1 Recall the story. Put a tick or a cross. 提醒学生回忆故事，观察第4至9页。

故事里妈妈没给艾文吃药。

故事里是伊森去看病，这是艾文。

2 Look at the pictures and discuss them with your friend. Have you had any check-ups before? 参考表述如下。

我的眼睛……不舒服，所以和他一样，也要……去看医生。

她的牙很疼，所以……她去看牙了。

他的身体不舒服，医生在……听他的心跳。

她可能生病了……

参考回答：
去年冬天我生病了，妈妈带我去看医生。/我身体很好，很少看医生。
讨论完后，老师总结：若身体不舒服，应及时就医。平时也应定期体检。

New words

1 Learn the new words.

延伸活动：
学生分小组看图说话，看哪一组说得好。如"蔬菜很健康，但是他讨厌吃蔬菜，所以妈妈很生气。""他不舒服，所以去看病了。他等医生和护士给他打针。""他生病了，妈妈给他吃药。妈妈说：'你应该多休息多喝水。'他的弟弟也在房间里，他很健康。"

生气

讨厌

医生

护士

看病

打针

等

生病

应该　药

健康

2 Listen to your teacher and point to the correct words above.

听听说说 Listen and say

第一题录音稿：
这几天，外公生病了，觉得身体不舒服。爸爸妈妈一起开车送外公去看医生。医生给他打针和吃药，还告诉他应该多休息。外公的病很快好了，健康回家，我们一家人很高兴。

03 **1** Listen and number the pictures.

04 **2** Look at the pictures. Listen to the story an

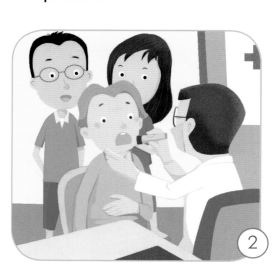

护士，请问我是下一个吗？

是的，你在这里等一等，很快到你了。

你的身体很好，非常健康。

太好啦！因为我天天运动。

1 What does the doctor say about Hao Hao's health?
   (He is in good shape, very healthy.)
2 Have you had any medical check-ups before? (Yes,
   I have medical check-ups every year./Yes, I had one
   two years ago.)

医生，我不喜欢生病，因为
我讨厌打针和吃药。

你还应该多吃蔬菜和水果，
知道吗？

我知道了，谢谢医生！

学生两人一组自由对话，完成后老师总结
"应该"的用法："人＋应该＋动作或行为"。

3 Role-play with your friend.

1 女孩的头很疼，
   她可能生病了。

   去看医生。

   她应该……

2 我明天要数学
   考试了。

   好好看书。

   你应该……

3 他们找不到火车
   站了。

   应该

   我们……
   帮助他们。

Task

老师先让学生齐读语段，并结合问题，了解如何描述生病的经历。然后两人一组，互相问答，再角色互换。最后可向全班同学表述自己生病的经历。

Look at the picture and read the boy's letter. Talk to your friend about a time that he/she was sick.

有一天，我的肚子很疼，身体很不舒服。爸爸妈妈送我去了医院，医生说我应该在医院休息两三天，还要打针和吃药。

我不知道我的病用中文怎么说，但是医生和护士帮助了我，我现在很健康。

你哪里不舒服？

你去看医生了吗？

谁送你去医院了？

医生怎么帮助你？

我……

Game

Play a doctor-patient game with your friends.

医生你好，我的孩子……

你哪里不舒服？不舒服几天了？

我……有……天了。

你……应该……还要……

好的，谢谢医生。

请等等，这是你的药，回家吃三天，还要多喝水。

Chant

延伸活动：
说唱后，老师还可以放《健康歌》
和学生一起边唱边跳。

🎧 Listen and say.

小朋友呀小朋友，
生病应该怎么办？
医生护士帮助你，
打针吃药多喝水。
爸爸妈妈帮助你，
多吃蔬菜和水果。
天天早起做运动，
身体健康快乐多。

生活用语 Daily expressions

真讨厌！
So disgusting!

请等等。
Please wait.

15

1 Trace and write the characters.

一 丁 丂 丌 丂 乇 医

丿 广 仁 生 生

医	生	医	生
医	生		

一 亠 广 广 广 应 应

丶 讠 讠 讠 讠 该 该 该

应	该	应	该
应	该		

医
生
应
该

2 Write and say.

我 应 该 多吃蔬菜，我不
应 该 讨厌它们。

我长大了想做 医 生，
因为 医 生 可以帮助
很多病人。

3 Read, circle the wrong words and write the correct ones. There is one mistake in each line. 提醒学生一边观察图片一边将段落完整读一遍，理解段落大意后，在每行中圈出一个错别字并在右侧横线写上正确的字。完成后，再通读改正后的段落，看看内容是否正确，文字是否通顺。

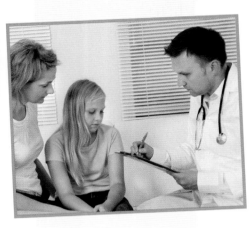

这几天，⊙找⊙觉得很累，也不   1   <u>我</u>

⊙相⊙吃东西，更不想去上学。妈妈   2   <u>想</u>

带我去看医⊙王⊙。医生说我生病了，   3   <u>生</u>

应⊙孩⊙吃三天药。   4   <u>该</u>

现在，我的病慢慢⊙孩⊙起来   5   <u>好</u>

了，我也开心多了。

拼音输入法 Pinyin input

Match the dialogue by drawing lines. Then type the whole dialogue in the right order.

答题技巧：
第一句"哪儿"问病症，应用"头疼"和"感冒"来回答；
第二句问症状的时间，故选"昨天上午……"；最后则是医生总结和病人表达感谢。

1	你哪儿不舒服？		好的，谢谢医生。
2	不舒服几天了？		我头疼，觉得很累，可能是感冒了。
3	你先吃两天的药，回家好好休息，多喝水，知道吗？		昨天上午还好好的，晚上开始头疼了。

多元学习 Connections

老师在介绍的同时，可通过互动增加学生的理解。如让学生按照针灸和推拿图中的穴位轻揉自己的手和脚，或模拟气功图的姿势做气功，然后说说身体有什么感觉。也可以让学生说说他们知道的哪些可食用植物有预防疾病或保健作用，如：大蒜能预防感冒、柠檬能减轻恶心、百里香能帮助消化、蔓越莓可减轻牙龈疾病等等。

Have you heard of traditional Chinese medicine? Learn about it.

Traditional Chinese medicine (TCM, 中医) has been practised for more than 2,500 years and has many different forms.

TCM is widely used in China and is becoming more popular all over the world.

Herbal medicine mostly uses plants. Herbs are grouped according to their effects on the body.

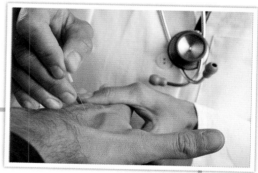

Acupuncture helps reduce pain and treats various medical conditions.

Qi gong is practised for exercise, preventive medicine and medical treatment.

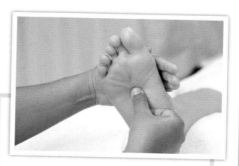

Tui na is a body treatment that gets the energy moving in the body.

Dietary therapy is based on the effects of food on the human body.

Project

老师告诉学生，"健康"并不是指没有疾病，而应该是生理、心理和社交三者都处于一种和谐、完好的状态。并且和学生一起讨论，还有哪些健康和不健康的生活方式。

1 Learn about healthy and unhealthy lifestyles. Which lifestyle is yours?

多吃蔬菜瓜果

多运动

保持心情愉快

熬夜、晚睡

常吃垃圾食品

健康的生活
Healthy Lifestyle

多喝水

勤洗手

不健康的生活
Unhealthy Lifestyle

心情忧郁

早睡

参考表述：
我再也不吃垃圾食物了，因为它们真的不健康。/ 我觉得我们应该多运动，还要多吃健康的食物和多喝水。

压力大

久坐不动

2 Talk to your friend to see if you have a healthy lifestyle. Can you give good advice on healthy living?

我放学后和哥哥一起去踢足球，晚上只看一小时电视。

我不坐公共汽车上学，我现在天天骑自行车上学。

我再也不……
因为……

我觉得我们应该……

19

1 **Complete the conversation and role-play with your friend.**

医 生，我的眼睛不舒服，很疼。

你的眼睛很红，是不是玩了很长时间的电脑游戏？

我从早上九点到下午五点在玩电脑游戏。

我给你一些眼药水，你的眼睛应该多休息。

小朋友，不要紧张，打针不疼的。

我讨厌打针！

你生病了，护士帮助你，你不 应 该 哭。

我会多运动，多吃蔬菜和水果，再也不天天玩电脑游戏了。

等你的病好了，我和你一起去跑步。

评核方法：

学生两人一组，互相考察评价表内单词和句子的听说读写。交际
沟通部分由老师朗读要求，学生再互相对话。如果达到了某项技
能要求，则用色笔将星星或小辣椒涂色。

2 Work with your friend. Colour the stars and the chillies.

Words	说	读	写
生病	☆	☆	🌶
看病	☆	☆	🌶
生气	☆	☆	🌶
医生	☆	☆	☆
护士	☆	☆	🌶
药	☆	☆	🌶
等	☆	☆	🌶
应该	☆	☆	☆

Words and sentences	说	读	写
讨厌	☆	🌶	🌶
健康	☆	🌶	🌶
打针	☆	🌶	🌶
我应该去看病。	☆	☆	🌶
我们不应该淘气。	☆	☆	🌶

Talk about physical health	☆

3 What does your teacher say?

评核建议：

根据学生课堂表现，分别给予"太棒了！(Excellent!)"、
"不错！(Good!)"或"继续努力！(Work harder!)"的
评价，再让学生圈出左侧对应的表情，以记录自己的学
习情况。

My teacher says ...

分享 Sharing

Words I remember

生病	shēng bìng	to be sick
看病	kàn bìng	to see a doctor
生气	shēng qì	angry
医生	yī shēng	doctor
护士	hù shi	nurse
药	yào	medicine
等	děng	to wait
应该	yīng gāi	should
讨厌	tǎo yàn	to hate
健康	jiàn kāng	healthy
打针	dǎ zhēn	to have an injection

延伸活动：

1 学生用手遮盖英文，读中文单词，并思考单词意思；

2 学生用手遮盖中文单词，看着英文说出对应的中文单词；

3 学生五人一组，尽量运用中文单词分角色复述故事。

Other words

感冒	gǎn mào	to have a cold
带	dài	to take
假装	jiǎ zhuāng	to pretend
病人	bìng rén	patient
紧张	jǐn zhāng	nervous
低头	dī tóu	to lower one's head
代替	dài tì	to replace
淘气	táo qì	naughty
生活	shēng huó	life

OXFORD
UNIVERSITY PRESS

Oxford University Press is a department of the University of Oxford.
It furthers the University's objective of excellence in research, scholarship,
and education by publishing worldwide. Oxford is a registered trade mark of
Oxford University Press in the UK and in certain other countries

Published in Hong Kong by
Oxford University Press (China) Limited
39th Floor, One Kowloon, 1 Wang Yuen Street, Kowloon Bay,
Hong Kong

Illustrated by Ah Lun, Anne Lee, KY Chan and Wildman

Photographs for reproduction permitted by Dreamstime.com

China National Publications Import & Export (Group) Corporation is an authorized distributor of
Oxford Elementary Chinese.

Please contact content@cnpiec.com.cn or 86-10-65856782

ISBN: 978-0-19-082309-2

10 9 8 7 6 5 4 3 2

Teacher's Edition
ISBN: 978-0-19-082321-4

10 9 8 7 6 5 4 3 2